Snore-dom™ BUSTERS

by Cindy S. Hansen

Group

Loveland, Colorado

Snore-dom™ Busters

Copyright © 1996 Cindy S. Hansen

Credits
Author: Cindy S. Hansen
Book Acquisitions Editor: Mike Nappa
Editor: Cheryl Adams Eisel
Senior Editor: Paul Woods
Chief Creative Officer: Joani Schultz
Copy Editor: Debbie Gowensmith
Art Director: Lisa Chandler
Designer: Helen H. Lannis
Computer Graphic Artist: Randy Kady
Cover Designer and Illustrator: Ray Tollison
Illustrator: Dave Bramsen
Production Manager: Gingar Kunkel

Unless otherwise noted, Scriptures quoted from The Youth Bible, New Century Version, copyright © 1991 by Word Publishing, Dallas, Texas 75039. Used by permission.

Library of Congress Cataloging-in-Publication Data

Hansen, Cindy S.
    Snore-dom busters / by Cindy S. Hansen.
       p. cm.
    ISBN 1–55945–706–6
    1. Amusements. 2. Indoor games. 3. Youth—Recreation.
   I. Title.
    GV1201.H367   1996
    793—dc20   96–8445
                                               CIP

10 9 8 7 6 5 4 3   05 04 03 02 01 00 99 98 97

Printed in the United States of America.

Dedication

To my sons,
Tommy, Steve, and Matt.
Life is never boring with my boys!

Contents

Section Two: Wild 'n' Wacky

Section Three: Romp 'n' Relays

Introduction

YOU'RE halfway through your meeting. You think it's going along fine, but you decide to take a reality check.

Uh-oh . . . Ben's eyes are at half-mast; he's on his way to lullaby-land. Chris has shredded a sheet of paper into confetti, and he's getting ready to blow it across the room. Tess is tapping Beth on the shoulder; she's got that "look" in her eye. If you wait any longer, you'll know exactly what mischief she's planning.

It's time to pull these kids back to the meeting. Quick! Who do you call? *Snore-dom™ Busters!*

Snore-dom Busters is filled with 106 creative, quick, easy, get-the-blood-flowing activities that get rid of the fidgets. And they require *no preparation.* The supplies are already in your classroom: scrap paper, trash cans, erasers, pencils, the ceiling, the floor . . . even the classroom door. It's never been so easy to bust kids' snore-dom.

These ideas will . . .
- add unexpected, action-packed breaks to meetings, retreats, special programs, and classes;
- refocus kids' attention back to the meeting;
- recharge kids' enthusiasm;
- build friendships and group cohesiveness; and
- show kids that church activities can be fun as well as faith-building.

Also, we've found that the smorgasbord of activities in *Snore-dom Busters* can work with kids from upper elementary to high school.

Questions About Interruptions

IT MAY seem odd to interrupt a meeting on purpose. After all, we try to avoid interruptions. But snore-dom busters are different.

These interruptions are intentional breaks in a program's uniformity or continuity. They're like commercials in your program that help kids refocus and re-energize. When kids are watching TV, commercials give them the chance to get up, stretch, and return to the tube renewed. In the classroom, these "commercial breaks" are even more important. They give kids the chance to get up, have some high-energy fun, and return to the lesson revitalized and ready to learn.

If you want to bust kids' snore-dom and add new life to your meeting, *Snore-dom Busters* is the book for you. Before implementing the ideas in this book, ask yourself these questions:

Should I interrupt? Sometimes you may think a program is flowing, but kids might think it's clogged. Take a closer look. Are they really interested in what you're saying? Kids have short attention spans. They need breaks and changes of pace to stay interested. If you've lost their attention, the high-energy activities in *Snore-dom Busters* will help them release steam and recharge their mental batteries so they can focus on the program.

Even the most colorful and exciting TV shows provide a break away from the action. In the classroom—where kids aren't glued to the tube and where we're competing for their attention—it's especially important to hook and rehook their interest.

When do I interrupt? Only you can know when to interrupt. Tune in to the atmosphere of the classroom. Look around. It's probably time to energize if you see or hear at least two of the following signs:

- eyes wandering or closed,
- blank looks in response to questions,
- kids slumped in chairs or leaning back with their arms crossed,
- chattering or whispering, or
- fidgety movements.

Won't kids lose their train of thought if I interrupt? Yes. And that's the point. Use snore-dom busters when kids' thoughts aren't focused on your topic. For the few who are focused, an interruption will energize them even more. Unlike adults, who may have trouble shifting gears quickly, kids shift energy constantly.

How do I get kids to refocus on the program when the activity is over? Simply state, "On with the show" or "Back to the program." You can briefly highlight the main points you've covered so far or ask kids to recall program highlights. The review reinforces what you've covered.

Do's and Don'ts About Interruptions

SNORE-DOM busters are planned interruptions. However, be careful not to let these interruptions become disruptions. When you interrupt your meeting, use the following tips to avoid disrupting it:

Be enthusiastic. Let your enthusiasm spread. Interruptions should be lively enough to brighten up a sleepy atmosphere.

Transition quickly. Get into and out of an interruption as soon as possible. Don't spend a lot of time preparing for the interruption. Be ready ahead of time. Know what interruption you want to use before you use it.

Make sure the activities are energizing, not alienating. Be careful not to put down anyone or make anyone feel inferior during the activity. We're children of God, so we should always "encourage each other and give each other strength" (1 Thessalonians 5:11).

Include everyone in the activities. Keep a roving eye for "hanger-backers" who are reluctant to participate. Some kids are more shy than others and need a little extra coaxing to join in.

If an activity calls for partners but your group has an uneven number of kids, you'll need to become a partner. However, if the activity requires an "instructor" and so limits your ability to be a partner, have the person without a partner team up with another pair or assist in the activity in some way. For example, that person could help you call out instructions or could be a "line judge" or "referee" during the activity.

Encourage cooperation, problem-solving, and teamwork. We're called to work together as the body of Christ. Teamwork builds community and friendships.

Choose teams in an edifying way. Never divide kids into teams by having team captains choose their teammates. This can leave the last-chosen few feeling unwanted and unappreciated. Here are some positive, identity-building ways to divide kids into groups:

- Divide according to favorite foods, color of clothing, birthday months, and so on.
- Have kids repeat a theme for the day, one word at a time. For example, if your theme is "Jesus forgives you," have all "Jesus" people form a team, all "forgives" form a team, and all "yous" form a team.
- Avoid forming teams according to height, weight, shoe size, or any other size or shape factor since this could embarrass kids, who come in a variety of all the above.

Modify participation for kids whose attire isn't appropriate for the activity. Do you want to use a snore-dom buster that involves getting on the floor or going outside in the grass? If so, you'll have to modify participation for kids wearing dress clothes. These kids can be coaches or cheerleaders.

Adapt the activities to fit your group size. All activities in *Snore-dom Busters* can be used in a small group. If your group has more than twelve to fifteen members, form more teams when necessary.

Use the activities to complement a retreat or meeting theme. For example, if you're studying God's love, the game Huddle Up on page 15 gives kids a quick "commercial break" that reinforces the topic. Or if your meeting theme is about materialism, the game Compact Condominiums on page 58 provides a new perspective on the material things in life.

So forge ahead. Read and enjoy *Snore-dom Busters*. Use it to bust snore-dom, re-energize your kids, and add unexpected fun to your meetings. ☼

Section One

Quick 'n' Easy

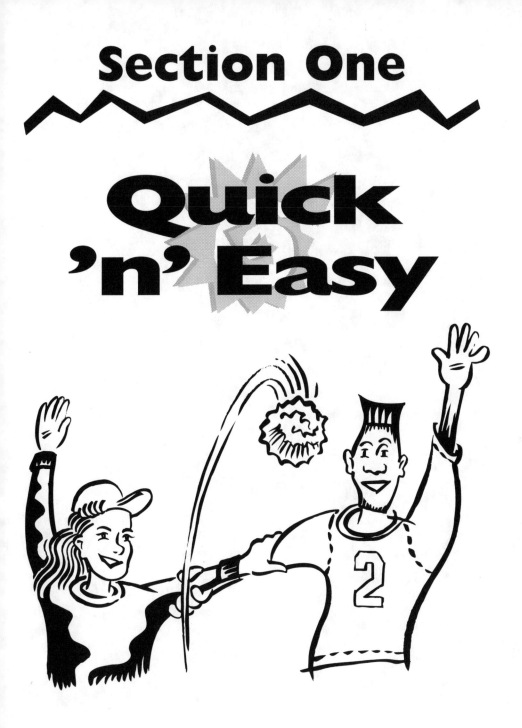

1 Whistling Dixie

WHISTLE AS LOUD as you can to get kids' attention. Then say: **Let's try an experiment. I'll point to one person, who'll begin whistling any tune as best as he or she can. That person must keep whistling while I point to another person, who'll whistle either the same tune or a different tune. We'll keep going in this manner until everyone is whistling. The only catch is that you can't laugh.**

See how far you get with this can't-help-but-laugh experiment. When everyone is whistling—and laughing—get kids' attention with another sharp whistle. Then go back to your meeting. 🌀

2 Huddle Up

WHEN YOU sense that kids need a picker-upper, stop the meeting and say: **Everyone form a huddle in the middle of the room.** When everyone is in the football-style huddle, say: **God loves you.** Have kids stack their hands in the center of the huddle and then yell "amen!"

Return to your meeting for one minute. Then call kids back to the huddle. When kids are huddled together, say: **God is faithful.** Have them stack their hands again and yell "amen!" Return to the meeting for one minute; then return to the huddle. Repeat this procedure several times, saying something different about God each time. When kids seem "picked up," have them sit down, and continue with the meeting. 🌀

3 Get Back, Jack

You'll need sheets of paper.

WHEN KIDS are getting antsy, stop the meeting and say: **Remember the game of Jacks that you used to play when you were kids? Well, we're going to play a game of Human Jacks.**

Have kids form groups of no more than six. Pick one person in each group to be the Tosser, and have the other group members be the Jacks. In each group, give a wadded sheet of paper to the Tosser, and have the Jacks huddle close together and face the Tosser. Explain that when you say "go," the Tosser should toss the paper wad high in the air and grab a person out of the huddle to stand by his or her side. The Tosser then has to catch the paper wad before it lands on the floor. If the Tosser grabs a person and catches the paper wad before it hits the floor, he or she gets to keep the Jack. If the paper wad hits the floor first, the Tosser must return all of the Jacks to the huddle and then start over. (See illustration.) Have the groups continue playing until all the Jacks are grabbed.

If you have time, choose new Tossers and let kids play again. Then get back to your meeting by saying: **Time to get back, Jack. Our meeting is waiting.**🌀

4 Stampede!

You'll need a pencil for each person.

IS YOUR MEETING being trampled by boredom? This idea will have your kids charging in the right direction.

Say: **Have you ever been told by a parent or teacher that you and your friends were so noisy that you sounded like a herd of buffalo? Well today we're purposely going to be that noisy; we're going to create the sound effects of a stampede.**

Have kids sit around a table, then give each person a pencil. Choose one person to be the Stampede Starter. Tell him or her to rub a pencil back and forth between the palms of his or her hands. Then point to the person to the Stampede Starter's right, and have him or her do the same thing. Follow this clockwise order around the table, continuing to point until everyone is rubbing a pencil. (This activity will be particularly noisy if kids are wearing rings.)

Point to the Stampede Starter again, and have him or her tap the pencil eraser on the table while the others continue rubbing pencils between their palms. Again, go clockwise around the table, motioning for each person to switch to this new motion.

Continue this procedure, having kids switch to the following motions: roll pencils back and forth on the table, lightly tap a side of their pencils on the table edge, then loudly tap a side of their pencils on the table edge. This is the peak of the stampede. Encourage kids to be as loud as possible.

Then have kids reverse the order of the motions: lightly tap pencils on the table edge, roll pencils on the table, tap erasers on the table, rub pencils between palms, then stop.

Say: **OK, we've survived the stampede. Now let's get back to our meeting.** ☀

5 Dream Vacation

INTERRUPT THE MEETING and say: **Let's take a break . . . and go on an imaginary dream vacation. Where would you rather go: to the mountains or to the ocean? If you prefer mountains, hold up your arms and say, "I love the mountains." If you prefer the ocean, make swimming motions and say, "Where's the beach?"**

Pause while kids respond. Then say: **Now find a partner who has your same preference.** (If there's an uneven number of kids, you'll need to participate in this activity.)

After kids have found partners, say: **Create a human "post-card" of something you and your partner enjoy doing while you're on vacation. For example, if you're at the beach, you could pretend to lie in the sun, ride the waves, or make sand castles. If you're in the mountains, you could pretend to hike, fish, or ride a horse. Whatever scene you choose, you'll need to "stop action" and hold the pose for a minute to share it with the group.**

Give kids a few minutes to practice making their human postcards. One at a time, have pairs show their postcards to the group so everyone can guess what's being depicted in the scenes.

After all the postcards have been shown, say: **What a great getaway. But now let's return from our vacations and get back to our meeting.** ☺

6 People Pack

SAY: Let's take a little break and get to know each other better. First, take a look at your shirt. Does it have buttons or is it buttonless? Now look around, and find others with similar shirts. All button-ups form one group, and all pullovers form another.

After kids have formed groups, have them take turns telling a shirt story. For example, kids could tell about where the shirt came from, if it's a favorite color or style, or why it has senti-mental value. The stories kids want to relate about their shirts have to reveal some insight about themselves.

Allow a few minutes for kids to exchange stories. Then have kids form two new groups: those who are wearing socks and those who are sockless. (If it's winter and most kids are wear-ing socks, form groups by light- and dark-colored socks.) Then have kids share socks stories. For example, kids could tell about their preference for wearing socks or for being sockless, a time they accidentally wore unmatching socks, a pet that likes to chew their socks, or a sock puppet they made.

Continue the activity by having kids form new groups according to who's wearing shoes with shoestrings and who's wearing shoes without shoestrings. Have kids tell a shoe story.

For example, kids could tell why they like their favorite pair of shoes or why they like or don't like to go barefoot.

Occasionally throughout the activity, shout: **People Pack!** Have everyone run to the center of the room to form a giant mob. When kids are in the cluster, have them tell a person close by something they learned during that particular story exchange, such as "Elaine tie-dyes her own T-shirts" or "Joe stumped his toe while going barefoot." After exchanging information, tell kids to return to their story-telling groups.

After kids have participated in the three story-telling groups, have them form one last People Pack. Say: **Now let's unpack and go back to our seats to continue with the lesson.** ⚙

7 Off-Key Chorus

IF YOU FIND that kids aren't paying attention in the middle of a meeting, say: **Let's stand, fill our lungs with air, and then fill the room with an off-key chorus.**

Have kids stand in rows, choir-style, and sing "Row, Row, Row Your Boat" off-key. Remind kids that this is their opportunity to sing horribly and to have fun doing it.

After the "choir's" ear-piercing performance, applaud kids' efforts, and have them sing another song...this time in their best opera-style voices, granny voices, or football-coach voices. Again, applaud their crazy performance. Have choir members take a bow and then sit back down. ⚙

8 The Unknown

You'll need a Bible.

STOP THE MEETING and say: **Follow me.**

With a Bible in hand, lead kids to an "unknown" part of your church, such as the basement, attic, or an out-of-the-way storage room. There, have kids form a circle and sit down. Say: **While we're in this unknown part of our church, let's take a moment to discuss your fears of the unknown.** Kids might mention family transitions, college or career choices, or upcoming school issues.

After everyone has had a chance to share concerns, pray for the courage to face these fears of the unknown. Then read Isaiah 41:13 aloud: **"I am the Lord your God, who holds your right hand, and I tell you, 'Don't be afraid. I will help you.' "**

Lead kids back to the familiar surroundings of the meeting room to learn more about God, who helps us face the unknown. ☺

9 Balancing Act

HAVE EVERYONE stand up. Say: **Let's try a balancing act. Stand on one leg and lean forward. Use your other leg for balance, but try not to let it touch the floor.**

Have kids hold this position as long as possible. While they're balancing, say: **Tell a person close by about some of the things you're balancing in your life right now. For example, you might be balancing jobs, schoolwork, church commitments, or family responsibilities.**

After a few minutes, kids will start losing their balance. Have each person who loses his or her balance sit down. When everyone is sitting, say: **No matter what we're balancing in life, God is our support. He'll always be there. Let's learn more about him.** 🔅

10 Spinoff

HAVE EACH PERSON get out a coin. Ask kids to lend coins to people who don't have any. Have everyone gather around a table or some other hard, flat surface. Then say: **We're going to have a spinoff contest to see who can spin a coin on its edge the longest.**

Have kids form pairs. (If there's an uneven number of kids, you'll need to participate in this activity.) Tell each pair to count to three and then to spin their coins to see whose coin spins the longest. Have each partner with the longest-spinning coin continue to round two, where he or she should team up with another person who advanced from round one. Have kids with the longest-spinning coins advance after each round. Continue until one pair is left to spin off for the title of "Coin-Spinning King" or "Coin-Spinning Queen."

After the king or queen is "crowned," have kids form a line for a royal procession back to their seats. Then move on with the lesson. 🔅

11 What a Mess?

You'll need paper and pencils.

GIVE EACH PERSON a sheet of paper and a pencil. Have kids make messy scribbles on their papers. Then tell kids to swap papers.

Say: **You have two minutes to add your own touches to make something out of the scribble. You could make a flower, a tree, a building, or something artistic.**

Call "time" after two minutes, then have kids show their scribble pictures to the group. Say: **Just as we made something artistic out of scribbles, God can take whatever mess we're in and make something good happen from it.** 🔆

12 Take a Break

You'll need a Bible.

SAY: **Everybody stand up and stretch. We're going to take a break . . . an exercise break.**

Lead the group in an exercise, such as jumping jacks. Then have another person choose and lead an exercise, such as toe touches. Take turns so each person gets a chance to lead an exercise. Tell kids that it's OK to duplicate an exercise if they can't think of a new one to do. (If you have a large group, you may want to limit the number of repetitions for each exercise so kids aren't doing dozens of each.)

When your turn comes again, have everyone jog in place. While kids are jogging, pick up a Bible and read 1 Corinthians 9:24. Afterward, tell kids to stop jogging and cool down by walking around the room. Say: **As you're walking, find a person close by and discuss these questions: What race are Christians running? What's the prize? You have one minute to agree on the answers.**

When a minute is up, have kids stop walking. Ask for volunteers to share their answers with the group. Allow a few minutes for discussion, then have kids return to their seats. 🔆

13 Yakety-Yak

You'll need a Bible.

SAY: **That's enough of our meeting for right now. Tell me about some of the things you've done this past week.**

Ask for a volunteer to stand and share a few of his or her experiences from the past week. Have that person continue to talk while you point to another person to stand and share his or her experiences. Tell the first person to remain standing and to keep talking while the second person talks. Both should continue talking while you point to a third person to stand and share. Proceed in this manner until everyone is standing and is talking at the same time.

Reverse the process by pointing to kids one at a time, having them stop talking, and then having them sit back down. When everyone is sitting, ask:

- **How did it feel trying to talk when everyone else was talking?**
- **How is this like trying to be heard and noticed in your everyday life?**

Pick up a Bible and read Romans 8:27. Say: **God is always here to listen to you. He loves you and cares for you. You're very important to him. Now let's get back to our meeting and learn more about our God who loves us so much.** ☼

14 Map Attack

IF YOUR KIDS seem bored with sitting in the same old meeting room, turn your room into a giant "map," and try these different "map attack" strategies with your group.

- Tell kids to imagine that the room is a giant map of the United States or North America. Designate north, south, east, and west. Have kids stand approximately where they were born. If they were born in another country, have them stand facing the direction of that country.
- Tell kids to imagine that the room is the state in which they live right now. Have them stand in the spot (outside their hometown) where they last traveled within the state.
- Tell kids to imagine that the room is a map of the Holy Land in Jesus' time. Have them walk where Jesus walked. Show them where Bethlehem, Jerusalem, and Nazareth were, and have them walk through those "cities."

Say: **No matter where in the world we stand, God knows where we are and is with us always. Now let's "travel" back to our room to get on with our meeting.** ☀

15 Scrappy Sack

You'll need several pieces of scrap paper and a trash can.

SAY: **Quick! Form groups of no more than six, then stand and face each other in a circle.**

Give each group a piece of scrap paper to wad into a ball. Say: **We're going to play Scrappy Sack. It's like Hacky Sack, but we'll be using a paper ball. The object of the game is to keep the ball in the air, bouncing it back and forth by using only your feet or knees. No hands are allowed. If the ball lands on the ground, use your feet to pick it up and kick it back into play.**

Allow kids to play for several minutes. To conclude the game, carry a trash can around the room, and have one person in each group kick the Scrappy Sack into the trash can. Then go on with your meeting. ☀

16 Field Goal

You'll need six to eight sheets of newsprint.

STOP THE MEETING and say: **Let's kick it into high gear and get some field goal practice.**

Have the kids form two teams. Have two people from each team create "goal posts" by standing side by side an arm's length apart from each other. Then have them grasp each other's wrists at shoulder height while positioning their free hands high in the air. (See illustration.)

Give each team several sheets of newsprint to wad into a big ball. Have each team member try to kick a field goal over the posts. Be sure kickers stand far enough from the goal posts to avoid any injuries.

When the game is over, applaud all the kickers, then say: **What a kick. Now let's kick back to our meeting and learn more about God.** ☼

17 Wait a Minute

You'll need a Bible.

IF YOUR KIDS look like they're about to fall asleep, say: **Wait a minute. I see some eyes at half-mast. Let's take a timeout to rest.**

Tell kids to lie on the floor, slouch in their chairs, or put their heads on their desks to take a rest. While kids are resting, read Matthew 11:28: **"Come to me, all of you who are tired and have heavy loads, and I will give you rest."**

After kids have rested for two minutes, say: **Let's get back to our meeting and learn more about Jesus, who gives us true rest and helps us with our problems.** 💮

18 Stash It—Don't Trash It

You'll need five grocery bags and a Bible.

ARE YOU WASTING your breath teaching a lesson that no one's paying attention to? Save your breath. Recycle your kids' attention. Say: **Time out! Let's take five minutes to search the church for items that people have thrown away and that can be recycled.**

Have kids form five groups, and give each group a grocery bag. Tell the first group to look for glass, the second group to look for aluminum, the third group to look for paper, the fourth group to look for plastic, and the fifth group to look for miscellaneous items (items that don't fit into the other four categories), such as pencils, erasers, or anything else that's reusable. Give kids five minutes to search the trash cans throughout the church and on the church grounds for recyclable items that fall into their groups' categories and to collect them in the grocery bags.

Gather kids together after five minutes, and have them report on their findings. Read Genesis 1:27-31. Ask:

● **What does it mean to be in charge of God's creation?**
● **How can we care for God's creation by recycling?**

Allow several minutes for discussion. Then say: **We must care for God's creation just as God cares for us. Now let's get back to our meeting to learn more about God and his creation.** 💮

19 Sensory Adventure

STOP YOUR MEETING and say: **I sense that you need a break, so follow me for a sensory adventure.**

Lead kids outside. Take a hike around the church, stopping five times. At the first stop, ask: **What do you see that you're thankful for?**

At the second stop, ask: **What do you hear that you're thankful for?**

At the third stop, ask: **What can you touch that you're thankful for?**

At the fourth stop, ask: **What can you smell that you're thankful for?**

For the fifth stop, go inside, gather by the water fountain, and let everyone take a drink. Ask: **What can you taste that you're thankful for?**

Say: **God has blessed us with many wonderful senses that we use every day. Now let's get back to our meeting to learn more about God's many blessings.** ☀

20 Follow That Ball

You'll need several pieces of scrap paper and a trash can.

HAVE KIDS form a circle. Wad a piece of scrap paper into a ball, and have kids toss the paper ball from person to person so that each person catches it once and tosses it on. Tell kids to remember who throws the ball to them and who they throw it to. For example, Tom throws the ball to Luke, who throws it to Ali, who throws it to Stephanie, and so on. As kids toss the ball, have them shout out the name of the person they toss the ball to. Have kids continue to toss the paper ball from person to person in the same pattern.

Wad another piece of paper into a ball, and have kids toss it in the same pattern while they continue to toss the first ball. Keep adding new balls. See how many paper balls you can toss at the same time in the same pattern. Then reverse the pattern's direction.

When you've had enough tossing (or the pattern gets too confusing), catch the balls when they come to you, and toss them into a trash can. Then say: **It's time to toss our attention back to our meeting.** ☼

21 Shoulder to Shoulder

SAY: **Do your shoulders feel tense from sitting? Let's take a break and do a little exercise to loosen them up.**

Have kids form pairs, and have partners face each other. (If there's an uneven number of kids, you'll need to participate in this activity.) Have each pair get out a coin. Ask kids to lend coins to pairs who don't have any. Have one of the partners in each pair place the coin on his or her shoulder while the other partner cups his or her hands as a target. (See illustration.) Each partner gets three tries to toss the coin, using the shoulder only, into the cupped hands. After three tries with one shoulder, have each partner try it again with the opposite shoulder.

Next have kids try tossing the coins with their elbows, allowing three tries per elbow. You can make the game more difficult by having the partner with the cupped hands stand farther away.

When everyone has had a turn at the elbow toss, say: **OK, now that we've worked some of the tension out, let's put our coins away and get on with the meeting.** ☼

22 Humdinger

IF YOUR KIDS are ho-humming, try this activity to get them up and running. Tell everyone to take a deep breath and then to let out a long hum. See who can hum the longest without taking another breath. Clap for the longest-lasting humdingers! Try it two or three times, applauding the winner each time.

Say: **Good job. Now everybody take another deep breath, and let's get back to our meeting.** ☼

23 Church Search

STOP THE MEETING and say: **You have two minutes to search the church and bring back something that reminds you of what we're talking about in our lesson.**

After two minutes, call the kids back together, and have them show the group what they found and explain how it relates to the lesson. Ask kids to vote for the most creative "church searcher." Retell the lesson using all the objects, then continue with your meeting. ☼

24 You Don't Say

SAY: **Everyone get one personal item from your pocket or purse, such as a set of keys, a comb, or a picture. Now form a circle, and place your item in the center of the circle.**

After everyone has placed an item in the circle, have kids scramble to change places within the circle. Once they're in their new positions, have kids form pairs with someone next to them. (If there's an uneven number of kids, you'll need to participate in this activity.) Say: **You have one minute to retrieve your partner's personal item and give it to him or her. You can't talk to your partner to exchange clues or descriptions. You can only mime what your item is.**

See how successful the silent partners are in searching and retrieving. Have everyone clap for a job well-done, then get back to the meeting. ☼

25 Catapult Capers

You'll need two pencils and two pieces of scrap paper.

IF YOUR KIDS are falling asleep, catapult them back into
action with this quick and crazy contest. Say: **Let's take a
break for some catapulting practice.** Have kids form two
teams, and give each team a pencil and a wadded piece of
scrap paper. Have each team line up along the side of a table.
Tell each team that its table will be its "playing field."

Say: **I want the first person on each team to stand at the
front of his or her team's table and position the pencil so
it's half on and half off the table edge. Lay the paper wad
on the end of the pencil that's resting on the table. When
I shout "catapult!" tap the other end of the pencil to send
the paper wad flying.** (See illustration.) **Then retrieve the
paper wad, and give it to the next person on your team so
he or she can try it. Continue in this manner until everyone has had a turn. Ready? Catapult!**

When the game is over, applaud all the contestants. Then
have the "catapulters" go back to their seats to complete the
lesson. 🔯

26 He Said, She Said

TELL KIDS to cross their arms in front of them. Then say: **If you have your right arm in front, find a partner who has his or her left arm in front. Keep your arms folded until you find a partner.** (If there's an uneven number of left-over-righters or right-over-lefters, have partnerless kids pair up. If there's an uneven number of kids, you'll need to participate in this activity.)

After everyone has found a partner, say: **Put on your best pantomime face, and silently describe to your partner something you'd never want to do. For example, you could pantomime breaking your leg, going sky diving, or robbing a bank. Remember, you can't say a word. You can only pantomime.**

After everyone has finished pantomiming, have kids form a circle with partners standing next to each other. Say: **One at a time, each set of partners will describe to the rest of us what their partner would never want to do by imitating their partner's pantomime. After each pantomime, we'll try to guess the action. Partners will tell us if we're right or wrong. We'll keep guessing until we've guessed the correct action.**

After everyone has pantomimed, applaud the performances, then indicate that everyone should take a bow. To get kids back to the lesson, motion "come here" with your index finger, and pat the seats of several chairs. 🌀

27 Symbolic Circle

SAY: **Look around the room, and find an item that symbolizes something about you. For example, a book could mean you like to read or a box of tissues might mean you're a sentimental person.**

Once everyone has found an item, have kids form a circle, and ask them to explain what their items symbolize. Then say: **God created us as unique individuals, but he wants us to work together as a team. Hold your symbols out in front of you with both hands, then face left. Step in toward the center of** the circle until you're so close to the person in front of you that your symbol touches that person's back. Now, with your left hand, place your symbol on that person's left shoulder. Then hold the item that is sitting on your shoulder with your right hand. (See illustration.)

Have the kids walk forward, rotating the circle in a clockwise direction. When they've completed a full rotation and arrive back at their original places, have them reverse the motion and walk backward, rotating the circle in a counterclockwise direction. When kids complete the full rotation and arrive back at their original places again, say: **We're a team of unique people, and we each have our own personality, likes, and dislikes, which are symbolized by the items we chose. Even though we're different, God wants us to work as a team. And what a great team we make! Now, as a team, let's get back to our lesson to learn more about God.**

Have kids break the circle, put their symbols away, and return to their seats. ☼

28 Thumb Wars

ARE YOUR KIDS twiddling their thumbs from boredom? Add some excitement with this thumbs up activity. Say: **When you walk by pop machines or phone booths, do you check for change in the change slots, or do you ignore them? Find a partner who would do the same thing you do.** (If there's an uneven number of kids, you'll need to participate in this activity.)

After kids find a partner, say: **Let's play Thumb Wars. Face your partner, and grasp right hands with your thumbs on top.** (See illustration.)

Say: **Count "one, two, three" as you move your thumbs from left to right to left. Then shout, "Thumb War!" Try to be the first to pin down your partner's thumb. Thumbs must remain pinned for three seconds; otherwise, it's not an "official" pin.**

Let partners play three or four times. Then say: **Thumbs up for a great game! Now let's give our thumbs a rest and return to our lesson.** ☉

29 A New Perspective

SAY: **I think it's time to refresh ourselves and view our lesson from a different perspective.**

Walk to the opposite side of the room. Have kids reposition their chairs to face you. Ask them to observe any changes in the surroundings. For example, the blackboard is now behind you instead of a window, or kids can now see into the hallway. Have kids discuss with someone nearby what changes they've observed and how they feel about this new view. After a few minutes of discussion, continue with your lesson from this new perspective. 🌀

30 Shield Me, O Lord

SAY: **Break time! Let's move our chairs to form an outline of a giant shield.** (See illustration.)

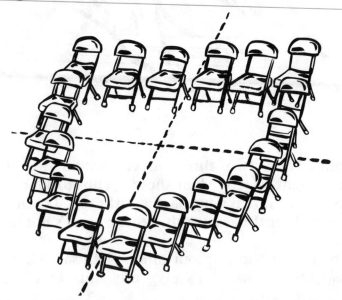

Divide the shield into four sections. Have kids form four groups, and assign each group a section. Say: **Each group will have three minutes to search the church for a symbol to place on its section of our shield. Section one will search for something that symbolizes what's good about our**

church—for example, a picture of our group doing community service. Section two will search for something that symbolizes an aspect of our church that few people know—for example, a trophy won by a church sports team. Section three will search for something that symbolizes our church's focus or outreach—for example, a poster of a mission our church supports. Section four will search for something that symbolizes how God views our church—for example a heart, cross, or Bible.

After three minutes, gather everyone together. Have each group place its symbol on the shield and explain to the other groups what that symbol means. Encourage group discussion about each symbol.

After all groups have presented their symbols, have kids take their seats within the shield and continue the meeting. 🌀

31 Scramble Bam!

HAVE KIDS FORM a circle. (For larger groups, form one circle for every ten kids.) Ask for a volunteer to stand in the middle of the circle. Say: (Name of volunteer), **point to someone and then start counting, "One, two, three, bam." The person you point to has to name the person on his or her left *before* you say "Bam." If he or she doesn't, the two of you will change places, and the person you pointed to must stand in the center. Occasionally during the game, I'll shout, "Scramble Bam!" When you hear this phrase, scramble and change spots with someone else in the circle.**

Play Scramble Bam for about five minutes. When you're ready to get back to the meeting, shout: **Scramble Bam—back to your seats!** 🌀

32 Pucker Power

SAY: We're going to take a quick break and have some **pucker-power fun.**

Have kids pucker their lips as if they've just tasted a sour lemon. Then have them open their lips just a bit to form a tiny "o." Repeat the pucker, but have kids open their lips to form a slightly larger "o." Continue this maneuver until kids form the biggest "o" they can. Then reverse the procedure, starting with the biggest "o" and ending with the smallest "o."

After kids have finished the last pucker, have them barely open their lips and whisper, "On with the meeting." Then have kids open their mouths as wide as they can and shout, "On with the meeting!" ☺

33 Take Me Out to the Ball Game

ARE YOUR "PLAYERS" dozing on the bench? Well take them out to the ball game. Say: **Everyone stand up and follow me. We're going to play some baseball.**

Have kids mimic your motions as you reach down to scoop up an imaginary ground ball and then hurriedly throw it to "first base." Say: **He's running . . . he's running . . . he's . . . out at first!** Pause for a moment, and watch in anticipation as the next batter steps up. Then jump high in the air to catch a fly ball. Say: **She's out—on a fly to right!** Again, wait for the next batter; then pretend to try to catch a pop-up by looking straight up to the sky and by staggering back and forth as you zero in on the ball. But wait! Bobble the ball and almost drop it. Then cup your hand over your glove to just manage to hold on to the ball.

If time allows, play a few innings. Then say: **Way to go, team! Now, back to our seats and on with the game ... I mean, the lesson.**

34 In Plain Sight

You'll need a Bible.

BEFORE THE MEETING, hide your Bible somewhere in the room. Make sure that it's in plain sight but that its hiding place isn't too obvious. During the meeting when you think kids need a break, say: **I've hidden an item in plain sight. In a moment, I'll give you clues as to what I've hidden. When you see it, tap your fingertips on the table** (or desks or chairs if you aren't sitting around a table). **We'll keep playing until all of you have spotted the item and are tapping your fingertips.**
Give these clues:

- **It's a very personal item.**
- **Most of you probably have one.**
- **Although it's not alive, it's full of life.**
- **It's not food, but it "feeds" many people.**
- **It doesn't make any noise, but it speaks volumes.**
- **It's a bestseller, but it's the least-read book in many homes.**

See how long it takes for everyone to spot the Bible. When all fingertips are tapping, retrieve the Bible from its hiding place and say: **The Bible is much more than just a book; it's God's Word. Let's continue with our meeting and learn more about the Bible.** 🌀

35 We Interrupt This Meeting

IF YOU NOTICE kids' attention lagging, interrupt the meeting, and have them do one or more of the following exercises.

- Place one hand on a chair, walk around it four times, then sit back down.
- Plug your nose and recite the ABCs.
- Laugh at least four different ways. (For example, kids could snicker, giggle, laugh like a cartoon character, or guffaw.)
- Peel and eat an imaginary banana.
- Talk with a foreign accent. ۞

36 Hard to Hold

IF YOU'VE COME to a hard-to-hold-their-attention spot in the meeting, you'll need a little lift to get over the hump. Say: **I can see that it's getting hard to hold your attention, so let's go outside and play Hard-to-Hold Tag.**

Lead kids outside, and choose one person to be "It." Then explain the game's instructions to everyone. Say: **I'll call out a hard-to-hold spot— such as an ankle, knee, or elbow—and It will have to tag someone in that spot. The person who is tagged becomes**

It and has to hold that spot until he or she tags someone else. Every few minutes, I'll call out a new hard-to-hold spot. OK, the first hard-to-hold spot will be your knee. Ready...set...go!

After the game, have the kids walk inside while holding one last hard-to-hold spot: the back of their left knees. Say: **Holding on to the back of your left knee, walk inside, tag your chair, then let go of the hard-to-hold spot.** Once inside, say: **Now let's sit down and continue with our not-so-hard meeting.** 🌀

37 Did You Hear That?

IS YOUR MEETING ROOM so quiet that you could hear a pin drop? Liven up the lesson with this activity. Say: **In a moment, I'll pick a person to be a Hearing-Test Coordinator. We'll keep our eyes closed while the Coordinator gathers four nonbreakable items, such as a book, pencil, eraser, and keys. The Coordinator will go outside our meeting-room door; then we'll open our eyes. The Coordinator will drop the items one at a time, and we'll guess what we heard. The Coordinator will tell us if we're right or wrong. We'll keep guessing until we've guessed correctly.**

Select the Hearing-Test Coordinator, then see how keen your kids' hearing is. Play a few times so kids can take turns being the Coordinator. After the last Coordinator has performed the hearing test, have him or her whisper—inaudibly at first—from behind the meeting-room door, "Let's get on with our meeting." Have the Coordinator continue to repeat the statement, getting louder each time, until the kids can hear what is being said. Then have them follow through with the directive by returning to their seats. 🌀

38 Miracle Maker

You'll need Bibles.

SAY: **It looks like we need a miracle to wake this group up. Everyone on your feet.**

Have kids form a line and count off by threes. After kids have counted off, have them form groups corresponding with their numbers. Ask each group to name a miracle that Jesus performed. (Each group should name a different miracle.)

Explain that each group will have three minutes to create a mini-skit about the miracle it has chosen. (You might want to pass out Bibles so kids can look up the miracles they've chosen.) Encourage kids to use "props" from around the room. When time is up, have each group perform its skit for the others.

After each performance, lead kids in a round of applause. Then ask for volunteers to answer the following questions:

- **What does this miracle tell you about Jesus?**
- **What does this miracle tell you about your relationship with God?**

After all performances have been given, end the activity with a prayer, thanking Jesus for his many miracles...not only those found in the Bible, but the ones he performs in our lives every day. ☺

39 Telescopic Vision

You'll need scrap paper, pencils, and Bibles.

ARE YOUR KIDS having trouble keeping their eyes open? Well, get their eyes back on Jesus (and your lesson) with this "telescopic" activity.

Say: **Everyone shut one eye. Keep your eye shut, and look around to find others who have the same eye shut. All those with their right eyes shut, form one group; all those with their left eyes shut, form another group.** (If you have a large number of kids, you might want to divide the two groups in half to form four smaller groups.) After groups are formed, say: **We're going to make "telescopes" to exercise our eyes—and to give us something else to look at besides the insides of our eyelids from dozing during the meeting.**

Give each group a pencil, then hand out a piece of scrap paper to each person. Have each group member take a turn using a pencil to punch a hole in the center of his or her paper.

After the papers have been punched, say: **Everyone shut one eye. Put the paper up to your open eye, and look through the hole. While you look through the hole, slowly move the paper farther away from your eye in one-inch increments. Notice how each time you move the paper, it changes your vision. Once you've moved the paper several inches away from your eye, slowly move it back toward your eye. Again, notice how each movement changes your vision.**

Wait a few minutes for kids to look through their telescopes. Then say: **Now, let's pay closer attention to our "new and improved" vision by reading Proverbs 4:25. First read the verse with the paper close to your eye; then read it again with the paper farther away.**

After the exercise, have each group discuss the difference between what they saw with telescopic vision compared to normal eyesight. Allow a few minutes for discussion, then say: **Now that our telescopes have helped focus our sights, let's refocus our sights on the lesson.** ☼

Section Two

Wild 'n' Wacky

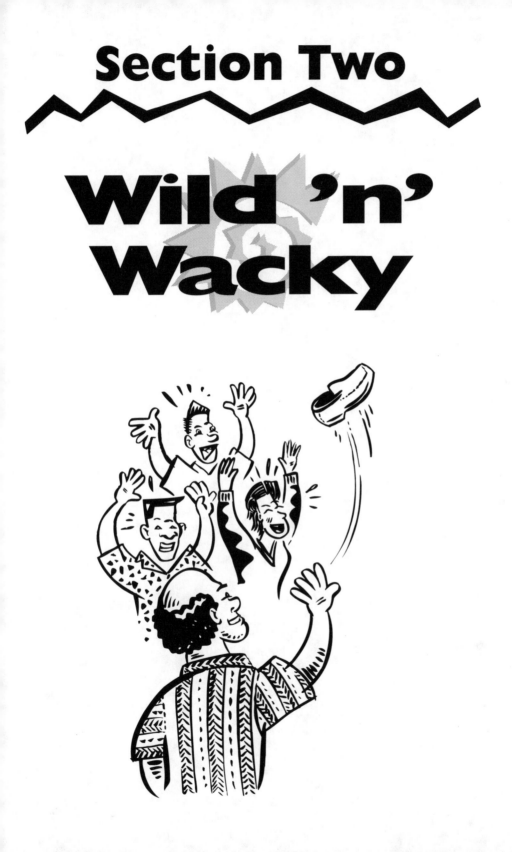

40 Light-Switch Bull's-Eye

You'll need black markers, scissors, masking tape, and newsprint.

IF YOUR KIDS' lids are at half-mast, try this eye-opener. Say: **It looks like we need a little help keeping our eyes open. So let's play a little game of Light-Switch Bull's-Eye.** Have kids form two teams, one team per light switch. (If your room only has one light switch, have teams make one target together and take turns using the light switch.) Give each team a marker, scissors, masking tape, and several sheets of newsprint. Then have each team stack its sheets of newsprint and tape them together to form one thick sheet. Tell each team to cut out a light-switch-sized hole from the center of the newsprint and then to draw three concentric circles around the hole.

Have each team tape its target to a wall, positioning the target so that a light switch fits through the hole in the center of the newsprint. Tell kids to move back to about five feet from the target and to mark the floor with a piece of tape, which will be the throwing line.

Ask one person from each team to provide a set of keys. Have team members take turns gently tossing the keys at the target in an attempt to hook the keys on the light switch and turn it off. (See illustration.) Let each person try three times.

After everyone has thrown three times, have kids applaud each other. Flick the lights on and off and say: **Great aim, everyone. Now let's take aim at a new target—our meeting.** ☀

41 Wacky Wave

HAS YOUR KIDS' attention drifted out to sea? Bring them back to shore with this Wacky Wave. Have kids form a circle with their chairs. Say: **We're going to do the "wave."** Create the wave by having kids stand up, raise their arms above their heads, then sit down, and lower their arms to their laps. Have kids complete the motion very quickly, one person at a time and one person right after another. For example, when the first person is standing, the next person should start to stand. When the first person sits, the second should begin to sit.

After the wave has gone around the circle a few times, reverse the direction for a backward wave.

Make the wave wackier by having kids raise different body parts, such as heads or elbows. For example, to create a "head wave," have kids remain seated, keep their arms at their sides, then bend over at the waist, and raise their heads in the air, wave-style. For a "foot wave," have kids remain seated and then raise and lower their feet to do the wave.

When it's time to get back to the meeting, say: **Great job. Now let's all take a bow . . . wave-style.** Have kids bow, using the wave motion, and then return the chairs to their regular positions to continue the meeting. ☀

42 Initial Blow

You'll need scrap paper.

GIVE EVERYONE a piece of scrap paper that's at least four inches square. Have each person tear the paper to form the first initial of his or her first name.

Say: **Take your initial and stand close to a wall. On the count of three, place your initial on the wall, start blowing** on it, and let go—keeping the initial on the wall by the force of your breath. Let's see how long we can keep our initials on the wall. Ready? One...two...three!

Have the kids repeat the exercise a few times. Then say: Now that we've gotten some fresh air into our lungs, let's get on with our lesson.

43 Close Squeeze

SAY: You're a great group of kids. Everyone works well together, and we're all pretty close. Now let's take a moment to feel the closeness of our group.

Tell kids they'll have one minute to squeeze into a closet and close the door. (You might want to survey the closet beforehand to make sure it's safe for this activity. Remove brooms, mops, buckets, boxes, or any other items that kids might trip over or that could fall off shelves in the commotion.) If you have a lot of kids, form two groups and use two closets. (If you don't have a closet in your room, try another room or hallway.) If you think your kids might have an aversion to squeezing this close together, especially in the darkness of a closet, then have everyone squeeze under a table or in the center of a prearranged circle of chairs.

Once everyone is squeezed in close, have kids say, "Thank God that we're a close-knit team." Have kids start "unsqueezing," and say: **OK, now that we've seen how close we can be, let's spread out and get back to our meeting.** ☼

44 Laugh-O-Meter

You'll need a Bible.

IF YOUR KIDS look like they could use a laugh, try this experiment in humor. Say: **Let's exercise our funny bones. Watch the position of my hand. When I hold my hand low, laugh or snicker quietly. As I raise my hand, laugh louder. When I reach the highest point possible, laugh as loud as you can.**

Raise and lower your hand to change the volume of the laughter. Have kids laugh softly and then work their way to laughing loudly. When you think kids have exercised their funny bones enough, lower your hand to the lowest possible position so the laughter turns to a light snicker. To end the exercise and silence the room, cross your hands in front of you to motion "cut." Then pick up a Bible, and read Psalm 126:2a: **"Then we were filled with laugher, and we sang happy songs."** Tell kids that the happy songs will wait for another day, and return to the lesson. ☼

45 Whirlwind Tag

LET YOUR KIDS burn off energy by taking them outside for this game. Have kids form three-person teams. (Four- or five-person teams are OK too.) Have each team's members form a circle, face to the left, and join right hands in the center; this forms the whirlwind. All teams will move with their whirlwinds throughout the game, moving clockwise and keeping their right hands joined.

Choose one team to be "It." Explain that when you say "go," all teams will run in their whirlwind formations away from the It team. If any member of the It team touches any member of any other team, that team will also become It and will try to tag other teams along with the original It team. Continue until all teams have been tagged.

To make the game more difficult, create larger boundaries. To make it less difficult, create smaller boundaries.

Repeat the game until kids are winded, then have everyone form a large circle and join right hands in a giant whirlwind. Whirlwind your way back to the meeting room for more of the lesson. 🌀

46 Up and Over

You'll need newsprint.

HAVE KIDS form pairs. (If there's an uneven number of kids, you'll need to participate in this activity.) Have half of the pairs go to one side of the room and the other half go to the opposite side. Use a row of chairs to mark a center line between teams.

Give each pair two sheets of newsprint. Have each pair wad one sheet of newsprint into a ball and place it in the center of the unwadded sheet. Have each pair hold the sheet by its four corners while keeping the paper wad in the center of the sheet.

Say: **When I say, "Up and over," use the sheet to toss your paper ball to the opposite side of the room. When a ball from the other team lands on your side of the room, pick it up and use your sheet to toss it back. You'll have two** minutes before "time" is called. The side of the room with the fewest paper wads wins. Ready? Up and over!

After two minutes, call "time" and count the paper balls. Applaud the team with the fewest paper balls. If time allows, play several rounds. Then say: **Now let's clean up and return to our meeting.** ☼

47 Whistle While You Work

GIVE A LOUD WHISTLE to get kids' attention. Say: **Let's take a break. We're going to have a whistling contest.** Have everyone form a circle, and have kids whistle to see who can whistle the loudest. Keep going around the circle, repeating the exercise and using the following ideas (or your own) to see who has the...

- softest whistle,
- longest whistle,
- most unique whistle,
- most birdlike whistle, and
- most ear-piercing whistle.

After each round of whistling, have kids applaud each other. When you're ready to go on with the lesson, give a loud whistle to get everyone's attention. Have kids whistle the song "Whistle While You Work" and return to their seats. ☼

48 Freeze Frame

SAY: **Everybody stand up and form a circle. You have thirty seconds to create a freeze frame of something you like to do. For example, you could pretend to be reading, eating, sleeping, or playing football.**

After thirty seconds, tell kids to release their freeze frames. Then have kids pose one at a time while the other kids guess their freeze frame. Once the pose is guessed, kids can "unfreeze."

After everyone is finished, say: **Now create a freeze frame of what you might look like when listening to a lesson.** Allow a few moments for kids to observe each other's poses (and to laugh at such poses as boredom, daydreaming, or sleeping) and then unfreeze the frames to get back to the lesson. ⚙

49 Shoe Fly

IF YOUR KIDS aren't paying attention to the lesson, try this little surprise. Take off your shoe, throw it, and shout: **Shoe Fly!** Retrieve your shoe, then say: **We're going to play a game of Shoe Fly. When I toss the shoe, stand up, clap, and cheer while the shoe is in the air. The instant the shoe hits the floor, sit down, stop clapping, and don't say a word.**

Toss your shoe several times using these ideas:

- long tosses for extended cheers;
- short tosses for quick cheers;
- high tosses for loud bursts of cheers; and
- slam dunks for explosive, momentary cheers.

Juggle your shoe for a few seconds as kids join in with cheers. Put the shoe back on your foot, and continue with the meeting. ⚙

50 Life's a Stage

ARE YOUR kids acting up? Then put them onstage. If your room has a window with a curtain or a blind, you have a built-in stage. If you don't have a window or if the window is not the correct height, your meeting room's door can become a stage.

Say: **Form groups of three by finding two other people who are wearing a similar color of clothing as you.** (Have kids who are wearing unique colors form threesomes. Four-person groups are also OK.) After kids are in groups of three, tell each group to create a pantomime about something they've learned from the lesson. One at a time, have groups go outside the window or door to perform their pantomimes. (For safety reasons, you might want to have an adult leader accompany each group outside.) When the group is in place, draw back the curtain or raise the blind, and have kids act out the scene. If you're using a door as the stage, have a group go into the hallway, shut the door, and get into position for the pantomime. Open the door when the group is ready to give its performance.

After each performance, have kids guess what message was being pantomimed. After all the groups have finished, do your own pantomime to say, "Let's learn more about our lesson." ☼

51 Quarterback Dash

You'll need a quarter.

HAVE KIDS GO outside and form two teams. Set boundaries for playing a game of touch football. For example, you could mark off the area with tape or put an object in each corner of the playing field. Say: **We're going to play Quarterback Dash, which is touch football using a quarter instead of a ball. The starting team will huddle and will pick someone to hold the quarter. This person will be the quarterback. He or she will try to dash to the end zone with the coin clenched in his or her hand. The rest of the team will also clench their hands during play so the opposing team won't know who has the quarter. The opposing team's members will try to tag**

everyone they can. When the starting team's members are tagged, they have to open their hands. When the quarterback is tagged, he or she must relinquish the quarter to the other team. Remember, this is *not* a contact sport. No tackling or collisions are allowed. We'll play for five minutes.

When time is up, applaud both teams. Have everyone huddle for a prayer, then go back inside to resume your lesson. ⚙

52 Highways and Byways

You'll need a Bible.

GET YOUR KIDS' energy back on track with this quick game. Say: **Let's take a different "road" with our meeting. We're going to play a game called Highways and Byways.**

Take kids outside to a grassy area that can serve as a playing field. Pick one person to be the Runner and one to be the Catcher, and have them stand on opposite sides of the playing field. Then have the rest of the kids form groups of an even number of your choice. For example, you could separate twelve kids into three groups of four. (Groups with uneven numbers of kids are OK, but even numbers of kids will work better.) Have the first group's members stand next to each other to form a row. Have the second group's members also stand next to each other to form a row, then have them stand behind the first group. Continue adding groups until all the groups are in line. Have the kids in the rows raise their arms out to their sides and keep them raised throughout the game.

Stand in front of the group and say: **This is the "highways" position. Whenever I say "highways," face me. Now turn to your right. This is the "byways" position. Whenever I say "byways," turn to your right.** (See illustration on page 54.)

Say: **The object of the game is for the Catcher to tag the Runner. However, the Runner and Catcher can only run within the rows formed—highways or byways. They can't run in between people or under people's arms. When I say "highways," rows will face me. When I say "byways," rows will turn to the right. The Runner and Catcher have to**

switch directions according to the row position. When the Catcher catches the Runner, the game is over. Ready? Go!

Play the game several times, choosing different kids to be the Runner and Catcher. After you've finished the game, read aloud Matthew 7:13-14. Then say: **The road to heaven is not an easy one, but it's the one God wants us to choose. Let's go back to the meeting room to learn more about God.** ☀

53 Get-to-Know-You Tag

WHEN YOU SEE kids' attention begin to lag, take some timeout for a game of tag.

Have kids go outside and then form two teams. Have each team form a line and face the other team by standing on opposite sides of the playing area. (You can make the game easier by decreasing the distance between the two lines or more difficult by increasing the distance.) Choose one person to be "It," and have him or her stand in the middle of the playing area.

Say: **This is a get-to-know-you game of Tag. Whoever is It will call out the name of a person who's standing in one of the lines. That person will then call out the name of a person who's standing in the other line. The two of them will try to exchange places before It catches them. If It tags someone, that person becomes the next It.**

Be sure kids know each other's names before you begin. If kids don't know each other's names, take a moment for kids to introduce themselves.

When the game is over, have teams walk past each other to exchange high fives. Then say: **Now that we've gotten to know each other a little better, let's return to the lesson and get to know God a little better.** 🔅

54 Rise and Shine!

WANT TO WAKE UP the sleepers in your class? Try this idea. Every time you notice sleepy eyes, shout, "Rise and shine!" Then have everyone run around the room once and shout, "I'm awake! I'm awake!" before returning to their seats.

Vary the actions each time you shout. For example, have kids run backward, hop on one foot, or skip around the room. Each time, have kids shout, "I'm awake! I'm awake!" 🔅

55 Rat-a-Tat-Tat

SAY: **Let's get energized by tapping out a tune with create-it-ourselves instruments.**

Tell kids they'll have thirty seconds to find something in the room they can use as an instrument to tap out the tunes of their favorite songs. For example, someone could tap a pencil against a heat register, clank a coin against a metal chair leg, twang a rubber band on the desk, or click a pen on a glass jar. Kids could also create instruments by using their hands and a table top— for example, drumming their fingers or rolling their knuckles.

After a few minutes, say: **Ahh! Music to my ears. Now let's continue with some food for thought by getting back to our lesson.** 🔅

56 Tightrope Tarzan

You'll need paper, scissors, string, masking tape, and markers.

IS YOUR KIDS' attention turned to something other than your lesson? All eyes will be on you when you pound your chest and let out a loud, Tarzan-like yell. Afterward, say: **OK, now that I've gotten your attention, let's play a game called Tightrope Tarzan.**

Have kids form two teams: Team 1 and Team 2. Give each team a sheet of paper, a piece of string, scissors, and a piece of tape. Have someone from each team cut a Tarzan figure—like the one shown in the illustration—out of the paper, punch a hole through the figure's hand, tie the string through the hole, and attach the piece of tape to the loose end of the string. (See illustration.) Have each team write its name on its Tarzan.

Lead the kids outside and find a tree. (If there are no trees near your church, draw a tree on a chalkboard or on newsprint. The tree should be at least four feet tall.) Tape both Tarzans to the bottom of the tree trunk. This is the starting position. (If the tape isn't sticky enough to hold the Tarzans to the tree, use tacks.) Place a piece of tape as high as you can reach on the tree's trunk. This is the finish line. Between the starting position and the finish line, place five pieces of tape equal distances apart.

Say: **I'm going to ask questions about today's lesson. Each time a team answers a question correctly, it will move its Tarzan one notch up the tree. There are five notches. If both teams answer a question correctly, both will advance.**

Ask easy, fun questions about your lesson until both Tarzans reach the finish line. Congratulate the kids on how well they answered the questions. Say: **See how much knowledge you retained from the lesson? What great students! Now let's return to the meeting room and learn some more.** ☀

57 Seek the Unique

SAY: **Let's take a break from our lesson for a "Seek the Unique" adventure. Find a partner, and let's go outside.** (If there's an uneven number of kids, you'll need to participate in this activity.)

Once outside, tell partners they have five minutes to seek out and find something unique. For example, a unique item could be a rock in the shape of a star, a four-leaf clover, or a leaf that looks like a face. After five minutes, gather kids together to share their unique "treasures" with the group.

Read Psalm 139:13-16, then say: **Not only are our items unique, we're unique too. God made each of us different from everyone else in wonderful ways. God is truly creative. Let's get back to our lesson and learn more about our creative God.** ☀

58 Foot Flex

IF YOUR KIDS are having trouble staying in their seats, get them on their feet. Say: **Let's exercise our feet. Everyone stand up and form a circle. We're going to do some foot flexes.**

Once in a circle, have kids stand on their right foot and flex their left foot five times. Then have kids stand on their left foot and flex their right foot five times. Have a volunteer count aloud as kids exercise so everyone is flexing in unison. Continue exercising, using these ideas (do each exercise five times):

● **Flex your left foot while toes are pointing to the right, then flex while toes are pointing to the left.**

- Flex your right foot while toes are pointing to the right, then flex while toes are pointing to the left.
- Rotate your left foot in a complete circle.
- Rotate your right foot in a complete circle.

Say: OK, now that we've done our foot flexes, let's "beat feet" back to our seats. ☺

59 Spy in the Sky

You'll need a Bible.

IF IT'S A NICE day, lead kids outside to a grassy area. Have them form a circle and then lie down with their heads in the center of the circle. Say: **Look at the sky. As you spot different aspects of God's creation, describe them out loud—for example, fluffy clouds, the shining sun, or different types of birds.**

After kids have described what's in the sky, tell them to shut their eyes. Say: **Imagine that it's a stormy day. What do you see?** Give kids a few minutes to describe the scene, then say: **Now the storm is over. Describe what's in the sky.**

Before kids get too comfortable lying in the grass (or fall asleep!), take them back inside, and read from Genesis about God creating the heavens and the earth. Say a quick prayer of thanksgiving, then go back to your meeting. ☺

60 Compact Condominiums

TAKE KIDS OUTSIDE, and have them form teams of no more than three. Say: **Let's test your construction skills. Work with your team members to build the tiniest building possible—a compact condominium. For example, you can build your condo with twigs, pieces of bark, leaves, pebbles, or any combination thereof. The only rule is that your building has to be at least five stories high.**

When everyone is done building, have an "open house" to tour the condo sites. Applaud all the builders for their fine

construction skills. Then say: **Let's head back to our non-condo meeting room and continue with the meeting.** 🌀

61 Face Contortions

HAVE KIDS FORM a circle so everyone can see each other. Say: **Let's take a break and make funny faces. For example, you could cross your eyes, make your nose look like a snout, curl your lips, do tongue tricks, and so on.**

After a good round of laughter, say: **No matter what we look like, God loves us. Let's get back to our meeting and learn more about him.** 🌀

62 Human Marbles

ARE KIDS so antsy that you think you're going to lose your marbles? Don't! Play Human Marbles instead.

Ask for a volunteer to be the Shooter Marble, and tell him or her to step aside for a moment. Have the rest of the kids form a close circle in the center of the room and then scrunch into marble shapes by squatting and wrapping their arms around their knees. (Kids wearing dresses or dress clothes can

be cheerleaders.) Kids should stay in a close circle while turning themselves into Marbles. Mark an imaginary border around the circle.

Once the Marbles are formed, have the Shooter Marble lie on the floor and logroll into the group of Marbles. Any Marble who falls over the border becomes part of the Shooter Marble's winnings. Then have all Marbles return to the circle, and choose a new Shooter Marble.

Play for five minutes, allowing kids to take turns being the Shooter Marble. Then have the kids return to their seats, and say: **Now that we've lost our marbles, let's get back to the lesson.** ☺

63 Circuit Training

TAKE THE "PULSE" of your group. If it's sluggish, get it in gear with this high-energy activity. Designate five stations around the room. (You can do this activity outside, but you'll need volunteers to carry and set up the chairs needed for certain stations.) Have kids form five groups, and assign one group to each station. Have kids rotate from station to station, performing the following actions.

- **Station 1:** Crab-walk in a circle.
- **Station 2:** High-step in a figure eight around two chairs.
- **Station 3:** Sitting on a chair, make rowing motions by bringing your torso down to knees, then raising your torso and pulling back your arms.
- **Station 4:** Do modified push-ups with your hands and your knees touching the floor instead of your hands and your toes.
- **Station 5:** Do jumping jacks.

Say: **You'll have thirty seconds at each station. When it's time to change to a new station, I'll shout, "Circuit switch!" Run once around the circuit training area and then go to the next station.**

Ask kids who are wearing dresses or dress clothes to be the Circuit Trainers. Assign each Circuit Trainer to a station, and have him or her encourage the athletes who stop there.

When everyone has completed the circuit, shout: **Circuit switch—to your seats!** Have kids run around the room one more time and then sit down in their seats to continue the lesson. ☼

64 Miniature Softball

You'll need paper, newsprint, and tape.

TRANSFORM your meeting room into a miniature softball field. Move chairs and tables to the sides of the room, then tape four sheets of paper around the floor as the bases. Wad a sheet of newsprint to use as a ball. Have kids use their hands as bats.

Have kids form two teams. Have one team play the outfield while the other team is up to bat. Use regular softball rules, but vary the way kids run the bases. For example, have kids run backward one inning, hop the next, then skip, gallop, and so on. Play three or four innings as time allows.

When it's time to get back to the meeting, say: **Now that we've exercised our bodies, let's exercise our brains by continuing with our lesson.** ☼

65 Untoppled Towers

IF THERE'S an imbalance in your meeting room—if more kids are acting bored than are paying attention to your lesson—try this balancing act.

Have kids form teams of four. Say: **Each team has five minutes to build a tall tower using stackable, unbreakable items that can be found around the room. For example, a team could stack books on chairs, boxes on tables, books and boxes on tables or chairs, and so on. If a tower topples, that team must start over and continue building in whatever time is left. Ready? Go!**

When five minutes is over, applaud all teams. Then acknowledge outstanding teams in the following categories:

- towers built with the most items,
- towers built with the fewest items,
- towers with the most unique features, and
- towers most resembling the Leaning Tower of Pisa.

Have kids race to return their tower-building items, then enjoy the rest of your meeting. 🌀

66 Crick-in-the-Neck Tag

You'll need scrap paper.

CHOOSE ONE PERSON to be "It." Give each of the other kids a piece of scrap paper to wad into balls. Say: **We're going to play a game of Crick-in-the-Neck Tag. Bend over at the waist, and keep your back as flat as you can. Place the paper ball on the nape of your neck, and try to keep the ball there while we play Tag. (See illustration.) If your paper ball falls off during the game, you must freeze where you are. You'll have ten seconds for another player to put the paper ball back on your neck so you can move again. It can run in an upright position with no paper ball, so you'll have to be quick. When tagged, you have to join It and help tag others. Once you are It, you can run upright with no paper ball.**

When you're ready to get back to your meeting, say: **Let's get rid of the cricks in our necks by getting on with our meeting.**

67 Musical Squeeze

You'll need scrap paper and a cassette or CD player with music.

ARE YOUR KIDS "marching" to the beat of a different drummer—one that's in some daydream—instead of focusing on your lesson? Get their feet going to the lesson's beat with this quick picker-upper.

Give everyone a piece of scrap paper. Have kids form a circle and place their papers on the floor in front of them. Play music, and have kids walk clockwise around the paper circle. Every so often, stop the music. When the music stops, kids must stand on the piece of paper closest to them. Repeat this procedure after removing a piece of paper from the circle. Then when you stop the music, two kids will have to share a piece of paper. Kids are never "out"; they just have to share a piece of paper with another person.

Play the game until kids are so tightly squeezed onto the few remaining pieces of paper that another person couldn't possibly squeeze in. Say: **What a tight squeeze! Now let's spread out again and get back to our lesson.**

68 Oh, the Nerve!

IF KIDS ARE BORED, "strike a nerve" with this activity, and get their adrenaline flowing.

Say: **People handle nervousness in different ways. Let's form a circle and see how each of us acts when we're nervous.**

After kids have formed a circle, say: **I'll start the ball rolling by showing you what I do when I'm nervous. The person on my right will go next. This person has to repeat what I did before he** (or she) **can show his** (or her) **nervous action. We'll continue to the right, with people repeating what all the others before them have done. By the time we complete the circle, we'll really know everyone's nervous habits.**

One at a time, have kids show what they do when they're nervous. For example, kids might chew on their lips, twirl their hair, crack their knuckles, tap their feet, and so on. To make the activity even more fun, tell kids they can exaggerate their nervous habits if they'd like to.

End the activity by repeating all the kids' motions. Then say: **This is making me nervous. Let's get back to the meeting.** ☺

69 Arm-Wrestling

You'll need a Bible.

SAY: **Everybody, think of your favorite dessert. Now stand up and walk around the room, saying aloud the name of your favorite dessert. Find a partner who likes the same dessert as you. Guys, find a guy partner; girls, find a girl partner.** (If there's an uneven number of kids, you'll need to participate in this activity.)

After kids find partners, have each pair sit across from each other at a table or desk (or lie on their stomachs on the floor). Say: **We're going to have an arm-wrestling match. The only catch is that you have to let your partner win. After one minute of wrestling, we'll switch arms and wrestle with the opposite arm.**

Pause for a few seconds while kids prepare for the "competition." Then say: **Ready, set, go!** After one minute, tell kids to switch arms. Again, pause for a few seconds while kids get into position, then have them wrestle for another minute. When the match is over, ask:

● **How did you feel during this competition?**
● **How is this like or unlike the way we should treat others each day?**

Read Romans 13:10 and 14:19. Say: **Remember to treat others with love and peace each day. Now let's return to our lesson to learn more about Jesus, who's our example of how to live.** 🔅

70 Huff 'n' Puff

You'll need pencils.

SAY: **Let's take a few moments to exercise our lungs.** Give kids pencils. Have kids form teams according to the number of tables in your room. For example, form four teams if you have four tables. Have each team's members line up at the end of its table.

Say: **When I say, "huff 'n' puff," the first person on each team is to blow his or her pencil across the table and off the opposite end. Count the number of blows it takes. If your pencil falls off the side of the table, place it back on the table at the spot it fell off and continue. Then the next team member will go. After all team members have gone, count the total number of blows it took. Ready? Huff 'n' puff!**

After the game, have everyone inhale and then exhale one final time. Then continue the lesson, refreshed. 🌀

71 On-the-Level Basketball

You'll need trash cans and newsprint.

TAKE TIMEOUT for a makeshift game of basketball. Place two trash cans on opposite sides of the room as two basketball goals. Crumple a sheet of newsprint as the ball.

Have kids form two teams. Have them play basketball with regular rules, except that instead of bouncing the ball, kids have to pass it after they take one step.

Play for one minute, then have two people hold the goals about four feet high. Play for one more minute, then have the "goal-holders" hold the goals above their heads. Play for one more minute. When the ball lands in a goal near the end of that minute, stop the game, and have the goal-holders put the trash cans back where they belong.

Ask teams to line up on opposite sides of the room in single file lines. Have them walk toward each other, and then have each person give a high five to each player from the opposite team.

Say: **Great game, players. Now let's continue with our great meeting.** 🌀

72 Hideaway!

CHOOSE ONE PERSON to be "It," then have the other kids divide evenly into two concentric circles. (If there's an uneven number of kids, you'll need to participate in this activity.) Have It stand in the center. Say: **People in the inner circle,**

walk clockwise; people in the outer circle, walk counterclockwise. It will count to ten silently, then will shout "hide!" People in the outer circle should then hide behind people in the inner circle. It will try to hide behind a person from the inner circle first. (See illustration.) **The player who's left without anyone to hide behind will become It and will go to the center of the circle.**

Play several times so several kids get to be It. Then say: **Enough hiding, let's seek out the rest of our lesson.** ◎

73 Impromptu Pingpong

You'll need scrap paper and books.

ARE YOUR KIDS bouncing off the walls with penned-up energy? Put that energy to good use with a game of Impromptu Pingpong.

Have each person find a book to use as a pingpong paddle. Then ask: **Which word do you prefer—"ping" or "pong"? Those who like "ping," put your hand on your head. Those who like "pong," put your hand on your nose. Now look around and find a partner who prefers the same word you do.** (If there's an uneven number of kids, you'll need to participate in this activity.)

Have each pair join with another pair to form a doubles playing team. Have each team create a "net" by placing two chairs together. Give each team a piece of scrap paper to wad into a ball. Players will use regular pingpong rules, but instead of bouncing a ball on a table, they must hit the paper ball in the air and over the net. Have partners take turns serving by rotating into the serving position after each round of play.

Play for several minutes. When it's time to return to the lesson, have kids put their paper wads into a trash can and return the chairs and books to their proper places. 🌀

74 Favorite Things

STOP THE MEETING and ask: **What sports do you like?** Wait for kids to give several answers. Then say: **Stand up and say aloud the name of your favorite sport several times. Find someone else who likes the same sport. When you've found a partner, I'll explain what to do next.** (If there's an uneven number of kids, let the partnerless person be the Questioner.)

When kids are paired off, have the class form two lines, with one partner from each pair in each line. Partners should be facing each other, and the lines should be at least five feet apart. Say: **I'll walk down the center of the two lines and will occasionally ask a question of a certain person. No matter what I ask, that person can't answer the question—the partner must always answer for him or her. If the person I question speaks, he or she takes my place and becomes the Questioner. I'll ask questions about favorite things, such as foods, movies, books, and so on. You might not have a clue what your partner's true favorites are, but that doesn't matter. Guessing or making up the answers will make the game more fun.**

Play the game until all kids have had a chance to answer for their partners. If possible, ask each person at least two questions. As a last question, ask someone:

● **What's your favorite thing to do at our meetings?**

Wait for the person's partner to answer, then have everyone return to their seats. ☺

75 Don't Laugh

You'll need a coin.

HAVE KIDS FORM two teams, and have the teams line up on opposite sides of the room. Appoint one team as Heads and the other team as Tails. With coin in hand, stand in between the teams and say: **I'm going to toss this coin. If it lands on heads, the Heads team has three seconds to laugh as loudly as it can. Meanwhile, the Tails team can't laugh or smile at all. If the coin lands on tails, the Tails team has three seconds to laugh as loudly as it can, but the Heads team can't laugh or smile at all. We'll play several rounds, using different actions.**

Toss the coin and begin play. When the round is over, have teams perform the following actions:

- crying,
- coughing,
- snoring,
- sneezing, and
- yawning.

When the game is over, have both teams cheer for each other as loudly as they can and then return to their seats. ☺

76 Crying Contest

You'll need a Bible.

ARE YOUR KIDS bored to tears with your lesson? Don't cry. Say: **Let's have a crying contest. We're going to go around the room, and one at a time, everyone give me your best weeping and wailing. People cry in a variety of ways. Let's try to demonstrate as many of them as we can.**

After everyone has "cried," have kids give standing ovations for the...

- most realistic,
- most unique,
- most heartbreaking, and
- loudest wail.

Read aloud Revelation 7:17b: **"He will lead them to springs of water that give life. And God will wipe away every tear from their eyes."**

Say: **Our tears today were fake, but there will be many times in life when they're real. When you face tough times, remember that God is only a cry away. Call on him, and he'll dry your eyes. Now let's get back to our meeting and learn more about God, who wipes away our tears.** ☼

77 Don't Do What I Do

DO YOUR KIDS seem unruly? Let them have some fun by "breaking the rules" in this game of opposites. Say: **Let's form a circle and play a game called Don't Do What I Do.**

When kids are in place, choose one person to stand in the center of the circle. Say: **Whatever actions the center person** does, we have to do the opposite. For example, if the center person hops on his (or her) **left foot**, we all have to hop on our **right feet**. If you forget to do the opposite and follow the center person's action, you become the new center person.

Before starting the game, help kids out by suggesting some of the following actions and opposite actions:

- **touch the floor and reach up high,**
- **stretch arms in front and stretch arms in back,**
- **stretch to the right and stretch to the left,**
- **bend over forward and bend over backward,**
- **wave right hand and wave left hand,**
- **raise left arm and raise right arm,**
- **raise right leg and raise left leg, and**
- **touch left foot and touch right foot.**

Encourage the center person to change movements quickly. Have several kids take turns being the center person.

As a last action, relieve the center person. Pull your chair into the circle and stand on it. Kids should do the opposite— return to their seats and sit down in their chairs. ⚙

78 Twin Artists

You'll need pencils and paper.

SAY: **Today we're going to exercise our creative brains. Everyone find a partner, then position your chairs so you're sitting back to back. You'll also need something like a book to put on your lap to write on.** (If there's an uneven number of kids, you'll need to participate in this activity.)

Give each person a pencil and a sheet of paper. Say: **Partners need to decide who will be the Artist and who will be the Twin. As the Artist draws a picture, he or she must describe it to the Twin so the Twin knows what to draw. In other words, the Twin tries to draw what the Artist is describing. You'll have three minutes to draw. When time's up, we're going to compare papers and see which set of partners comes closest to having twin pictures. Then we'll switch roles.**

After three minutes, have kids compare papers. Then have partners turn their papers over and switch roles so the Twin becomes the Artist and vice versa. Tell kids they must think of a new picture to draw; they can't draw the same thing they drew in the first round. Allow three minutes for partners to draw, then compare papers again.

Have kids place their chairs back in their normal positions, and say: **There's an artist in each of us. All we have to do is find our creativity. Now let's get back to our meeting and learn more about the most creative artist of all time, God.** ☀

79 Gone Fishing

You'll need paper, pencils, and Bibles.

WOULD YOUR KIDS rather be fishing than attending your meeting? Maybe you need a new angle. Try this lure on your group.

Have kids form groups of four or five. Have each group select a Fishing Guide. Gather Guides around a table, and give each Guide a sheet of paper. (To keep the rest of the group busy while you're providing instructions to the Guides, give each group a Bible, and have kids read Luke 5:1-7 and John 21:1-13.) Tell each Guide to fold the paper in thirds lengthwise and then in thirds widthwise to create nine even squares over the entire face of the paper. Have Guides repeat this procedure to reinforce the folds. Give each Guide a pencil, and have him or her draw a fish in the center square. Then have each Guide tear his or her paper into the nine squares.

To the Guides only, say: **Turn your squares over so you can't see which one has the fish on it. Now shuffle the squares around on the table so you're really unsure which is which. Can you pick the fish?** Give each Guide a few chances to try to choose the square with the fish, then reveal the "secret": The square with the fish has four torn edges because it was the center square. The other squares have at least one side that is the straight, undamaged edge of the paper. To find the fish, a person must look for the square with four torn sides.

Have the Guides return to their groups to repeat this fishy

trick. (You might want to talk the Guides through the proce-dure as they're sharing it with others.) Tell the Guides to first turn all the squares up so group members can see that only one square has a fish on it. Then have the Guides turn the squares with the fish over. Then have them shuffle the squares around and let group members take turns trying to pick the square with the fish. After everyone has had a turn, have the Guides reshuffle and—knowing the secret of the four torn sides—immediately pick the fish from the rest of the squares. (Guides might want to reshuffle and repeat the trick to show that their pick wasn't just the "luck of the draw." Also, if a group member knows the trick, have the Guide tell him or her to keep the secret until everyone has had a chance to try to choose the square with the fish.)

Once the secret is revealed, have kids return to their seats as you read aloud Luke 5:1-7. ☼

80 Bark in the Dark

IF YOUR KIDS seem more like "sleeping dogs" than attentive students, they're sure to get a howl out of this activity. Turn out the lights, pull down the blinds, and have a Bark in the Dark contest.

Have kids form a wide circle facing outward so they can't see each other's faces. Call out the following barks, and go around the circle, letting each person take a turn performing the barks:

- loud bark,
- soft bark,
- mean bark,
- happy bark,
- stepped-on-a-sticker-bush bark,
- big dog bark,
- little dog bark, and
- all-around goofiest bark.

Then open the shades, turn on the lights, and have kids face the center of circle. One at a time, have them perform their favorite bark so others can see who was barking in the dark. After the last person has barked, have kids return to their seats while barking to the tune of "How Much Is That Doggie in the Window?"

Section Three

Romp 'n' Relays

81 If the Coin Fits, Wear It

SAY: **On your feet! Time for a relay!** Have kids form teams of four. Tell kids that each team will need a coin—any coin will do. Ask kids to lend coins to teams who don't have any. Once teams are formed, have team members lie side by side on the floor. (Kids wearing dresses or dress clothes can be line judges and oversee the relay.) Tell team members to turn their heads to face the first person on their teams so they'll know when it's their turn.

Say: **The first person on each team will place the coin in the center of his or her forehead. He or she can use only facial movements, such as eyebrow wiggles or nose scrunches, to move the coin off the forehead and onto the floor. Shaking the head to make the coin fall off is not allowed. Once the coin is on the floor, the second team member will place the coin on his or her forehead and will also try to wiggle it off. The third and fourth team members will follow suit.**

During the relay, line judges can check to make sure that coins are being placed in the center of kids' foreheads and that kids use only facial muscles to move the coins.

When the relay is over, applaud all teams. If time allows, play again, but vary the game by having kids place the coins on other places on their faces, such as in the space between their noses and upper lips or on their chins. 🔆

82 Human Hoop Shoot

You'll need newsprint.

HAVE KIDS form teams of four. Then have kids create team "basketball goals" by having one person on each team hold out his or her arms in a hoop-shaped circle. Give a piece of newsprint to each team to wad into a ball.

Say: **Your team has one minute to shoot hoops. Rotate shooting so that everyone gets one shot before moving on to the next player.**

When a minute is up, call time and applaud the players. Play again, but have different kids form the hoops. Play as long as time allows, then return to the meeting. ☺

83 Stunt Relay

HAVE KIDS FORM teams of no more than six people. Go outside to a grassy area, and have teams line up on one side of the area.

Tell kids to think of physical stunts to do, such as cartwheels, forward rolls, logrolls, etc. (Kids wearing dresses or dress clothes could do stunts such as hop backward on one foot or close their eyes and pretend to walk on a tightrope.) One at a time, have team members perform their stunts while moving forward across the playing field. Once a person completes the stunt, the next team member will race out to where that person stopped, and he or she will perform another stunt, continuing to move across the playing field. For example, one team member could do a forward roll, the next person could walk on his or her hands, the next could do a standing broad jump, and so on until all team members have taken a turn.

After everyone has taken a turn, have kids perform one final stunt in unison by jumping in the air, clapping, and cheering for each other. Then lead the group back inside for more of the lesson. ☺

84 Strung Along

You'll need scissors and masking tape.

ARE YOUR KIDS "stringing you along" by pretending to pay attention? Get them back into the lesson with this fun exercise. Lead kids outside to a grassy area. (Don't forget to bring the scissors and masking tape.) Once outside, say: **Look down at your feet. Those of you without shoestrings, come up and get some tape.** Give each "shoestringless" person a two-foot piece of masking tape. After the tape has been handed out, have everyone stand side by side, forming a line on one side of the playing field. Choose someone to be the Leader, and tell him or her *not* to follow the instructions you give to the rest of the group.

Turn to the group and say: **For those of you with shoestrings, tie the inside halves of your shoestrings together so your shoes are connected. Then tie the outside halves of your shoestrings to the shoestrings of the people standing on either side of you. For those of you without shoestrings, wrap the tape around both ankles so your ankles are connected to each other. Then wrap the ends of the tape to the shoestrings of the people standing next to you.**

Ask for three volunteers—two with shoestrings and one without—to demonstrate. Have the person without shoestrings stand in the middle. Have the volunteers tie themselves together as described. (See illustration.)

After kids are strung together, point to the opposite side of the field and say: **All of you who are tied together will follow the Leader. The Leader will take the hand of the first person in line and will quickly guide the rest of you across the field. You must stay in line during the race and trust your fearless Leader to guide you to the finish line. Move quickly but carefully! If your strings become untied, retie them. If you're using tape and it breaks, scrunch it back together the best you can. The point is that you must continue the race. Ready? Go!**

After everyone has reached the finish line, congratulate kids on their speed and agility, and give them a few moments to catch their breaths. Then have the Leader guide everyone back across the field. After the race is finished, give everyone a big round of applause. Then have the Leader guide the tied-together kids back to the meeting area. ⚙

85 Where's My Chair?

HAVE KIDS FORM two teams: Team 1 and Team 2. Have teams stand on opposite sides of the room. Give Team 1 two chairs. (For safety reasons, don't use folding chairs.) Appoint a Spotter for each team to prevent kids who lose their balance from falling off the chairs. (Kids wearing dresses or dress clothes would make good Spotters.)

Say: **When I say, "Where's my chair?" the first player from Team 1 will step from chair to chair, moving the chairs as he or she goes along, to get to the other side of the room. (See illustration.) As players cross with the chairs, they can't touch the floor. If they touch the floor, they have to wait**

three seconds before resuming. When a player reaches the other side, a member of Team 2 will reverse the process by

stepping from chair to chair, moving the chairs back across the room. This procedure will continue until everyone from one side of the room is on the other side. Ready? Where's my chair?

When the race is over, give everyone a cheer. Have kids return all chairs to their normal positions, and go on with the lesson.

 86 Double-Jointed

You'll need a Bible.

IF SOME of the "bodies" in your class are "disjointed" or distracted, this activity will have them working together in no time.

Read aloud Ephesians 4:16, then say: **Let's have a partner race and see what it's like to be joined together when we run. First, let's form partners. How many of you put on a sweatshirt by sticking your head through first? How many put your arms in first? Find a partner who puts on a sweatshirt the same way you do.** (If there's an uneven number of kids, you'll need to participate in this activity.)

Have kids stand next to their partners on one side of the room. Say: **The object of this relay is for partners to get to the other side of the room, walking as quickly as possible. To begin the race, I'll call out two body joints that you and your partner will put together as you walk. Throughout the race, I'll call out different joint connections. You have to change joint connections and keep going. Ready? Finger joint to elbow joint!**

Several times during the race, shout out new joint connections, such as elbow to knee, knee to wrist, wrist to shoulder, and so on. After the race is over, have kids discuss why it's sometimes hard to work together to be the body of Christ. Allow a few minutes for discussion, then say: **With God's help, all things are possible. Now let's get back to the lesson and learn more about God.**

87 Corner Ball

You'll need scrap paper.

HAVE KIDS FORM four teams, and assign each team a corner of the room's ceiling. Give each team a piece of scrap paper to wad into a ball.

Say: **Team members will take turns trying to hit the exact ceiling corner with the paper ball. The catch is that whoever is shooting has to close his or her eyes. Each time someone on your team makes a direct hit, give him or her a round of applause. We'll play for two minutes. Ready? Go!**

When the game is over, let the kids play again; this time, let them shoot with their eyes open. When it's time to get back to the lesson, have kids throw away the paper balls and return to their seats. ☺

88 Backpack Relay

SAY: **It seems like we're carrying a heavy load today. Let's try to take some of that weight off our shoulders.**

Have kids form two teams. Have half of each team stand on opposite sides of the room. Say: **Choose a lightweight person from your team to be the Backpack. Choose another person to be the Carrier. The Backpack and the Carrier will stand back to back and will hook elbows. The Carrier will bend forward slightly so that the Backpack's feet come off the floor. The Carrier will carry the Backpack to the opposite side of the room and will set him or her down. Then a Carrier from that side of the room will carry the Backpack back to the original side. Each team will continue until everyone has carried the Backpack.**

When the relay is over, say: **Now that we've lightened our loads, let's "backpack" on with our lesson.** ☺

89 Staying Put

You'll need pencils.

IF YOUR LESSON needs a lift, try this elevating activity. Have kids form teams of no more than four, and give each team a pencil. Say: **What is the highest spot in this room where we can lay a pencil so it stays put? We're going to race to find that spot. You'll have three minutes. Ready? Go!**

When time is up, inspect all spots to see which is the highest. Then say: **Now, where's the lowest spot in the room where we can lay a pencil so it stays put? The floor doesn't count. This time, you have only one minute. Ready? Go!**

Again, when time is up, inspect all spots to see which is the lowest. Have a volunteer collect the pencils, then return to the lesson.

90 Air Show

You'll need paper.

GIVE KIDS PAPER, and have each person fold a paper airplane. Say: **Now that we've made planes, let's take a moment to enjoy an air show. With our squadron of sharp fliers, we're sure to put on a memorable exhibition.**

Have kids take turns to see who can perform these highflying stunts:

- longest flight,
- shortest flight,
- smoothest takeoff,
- roughest landing,
- highest altitude,
- bumpiest route,
- biggest loop-the-loop,
- widest zigzag, and
- most creative flight pattern.

Encourage a lot of "oohs" and "aahs" during the performances. End the exhibition by having all the kids aim their airplanes for a direct landing in a trash can. 🌀

91 Off the Wall

You'll need newsprint.

ARE YOUR KIDS climbing the walls? To relieve some tension, try this "Off the Wall" relay. Have kids line up about five feet from a wall. Give the first person a sheet of newsprint to wad into a ball.

Say: **The first person will toss the paper ball against the wall, and the second person will have to catch it before it hits the ground. Then the second person will toss it against the wall, and the third person will have to catch it before it hits the ground. We'll continue until everyone has tossed and caught the ball. If someone drops the ball, he or she must retrieve the ball, give it back to the thrower, then try again.**

Applaud the off-the-wall relayers, then move on with your meeting. 🌀

92 Squat-a-Lot Relay

HAVE KIDS DIVIDE evenly into teams of no more than four. Tell each team to find a "throwable" item, such as a note pad or comb. Have each team form a line. Designate the first person in each line as the Tosser. Have each Tosser hold the item and face the rest of his or her group.

Say: **When I say, "Squat a lot," each Tosser will toss the item to the first person in line, who will toss it back and then squat down. Then the Tosser will throw the item to the second person, who will toss it back and squat down. The Tosser will then toss the item to the third person (who is the last person in line), and he or she will toss it back to the Tosser and remain standing. This time when the Tosser catches the item, he or she will step forward and squat down at the front of the line. Once the Tosser is squatting, the last person will climb over all the squatting bodies and go to the front to become the new Tosser. (See illustration.) We'll play until everyone has been the Tosser.** (Kids wearing dresses or dress clothes could be cheerleaders.) **Any questions? Ready? Squat a lot.**

When the relay is over, applaud all "squatters," then return to the meeting. 🌀

93 A-MAZE-ing

SAY: **We seem a little sidetracked today, and I don't want us to hit a dead end with this lesson. So let's take a different direction.**

Have kids form two teams. Assign each team half of the room. (If your room is small, use a larger room or go outside.) Say: **You have three minutes to make a maze for the other team to crawl through. You can use chairs, tables, boxes—whatever you can find—as long as the maze is not impossible or dangerous to navigate. After the mazes have been built, each team will race through the other team's maze.**

After three minutes, halt the production of the mazes. Have each team race through the other team's maze. When teams have finished the race, have them applaud each other. Ask:

● **How was maneuvering through the mazes similar to maneuvering through life as Christians?**

Allow several minutes for discussion, then say: **God has blessed us with an "a-maze-ing" group. Now let's get back to our meeting to learn more about God.** ☼

94 Erase-Track Relay

You'll need pencils and chalkboard erasers.

GIVE EACH PERSON two pencils—one to hold in each hand. Have kids form two teams, and have both teams line up on one side of the room. Place two chairs on the opposite side of the room. Put a chalkboard eraser on the floor in front of the first person on each team.

Say: **This is a kneeling relay, so everyone down on your knees.** (Pause while kids kneel.) **On "go," the first person on each team will use the pencils to pick up the eraser. He or she will then carry the eraser across the room, around the chair, back to his or her team, and will then pass the eraser to the next person. The next person will repeat the procedure. When transferring the eraser to the next person, you must** use the pencils. You can't touch the eraser with any part of your body. If you drop the eraser or pencils, go back to your position in line and start over. Ready to race? Go! (Kids wearing dresses or dress clothes could be line judges or cheerleaders.)

Have kids click their pencils together and shout encouragement while their team members race.

After the relay, have kids form a circle and touch pencil tips in the center of the circle. Have everyone shout, "Good job!" Then break the huddle and get back to the meeting. ☼

95 That's Using Your Head

You'll need newsprint.

HAVE THE KIDS divide evenly into two teams, and have both teams line up on one side of the room. Have the first and last person in each line become partners, the second person and second-to-last become partners, and so on until everyone has a partner. (If there's an uneven number of kids, you'll need to participate in this activity.)

After kids have paired up, say: **We're going to have a relay that really uses our heads. I need two pairs to demonstrate.**

Have one pair stand a foot apart, facing each other. Place a wadded sheet of newsprint between their foreheads, and tell them to press their foreheads together to keep the wad in place. Say: **Use your heads!** Then have the pair walk sideways across the room and back. Before they return, have the second pair move forward and cup their hands together to form one large cup. When the first pair returns, have them come to a stop over the second pair's hands and then separate foreheads so the paper wad drops into the cupped hands. (See illustration.) Then have a person from the first pair pick up the paper wad and place it between the second pair's foreheads so the second pair can walk across the room.

Say: **During the relay, each pair must transfer the paper wad to the next pair in the way that was demonstrated. The relay pair cannot touch the paper wad with their own hands at any time during the race. They can only touch the paper once they've dropped it into the next pair's**

hands. If the relay partners drop the paper during the race, they can't pick it up. The next pair on their team must run to assist them. We'll race until all participants have used their heads. **Any questions?**

When both teams are ready, say: **Use your heads!**

When the relay is over, applaud all participants. Throw the paper wads in the trash can, then say: **Way to go! You really used your heads! Now let's use our heads to learn more about God. Time to return to our lesson.** ☼

96 **The Nose Knows**

ARE YOUR KIDS snoring? Put their noses to better use with this snore-dom buster. Have kids form two teams, and have both teams line up on one side of the room. Say: **When I say, "Oh nose," the first person on each team will hold his or her right nostril closed while quickly walking across the room and back. Then the next member of each team will walk while holding his or her right nostril closed. Continue until everyone on your team has walked this way. Ready? Oh nose!**

When the relay is over, applaud all the contestants. Have kids take a deep breath with both nostrils, then continue the meeting. ☼

97 Cone Ball

You'll need scrap paper.

GIVE EACH PERSON a sheet of scrap paper to roll into a cone shape. Have kids form two teams. Have each team line up with team members spaced three feet apart. Give the first person on each team a wadded piece of scrap paper to place inside their cone.

Say: **On "go," the first team member will toss the ball into the next team member's cone. That person will toss it into the next member's cone, and so on. Toss the ball all the way down the line and then back to the front again. When the ball is back in the first person's cone, everyone on that team should yell, "Cone ball!" and sit down.**

If time allows, play another round with kids passing the ball. When the relay is over and everyone is sitting, ask kids if they'd like to remain where they are or return to their seats to continue with the lesson. 🌀

98 At the Drop of a Stick

You'll need two yardsticks (or mops or brooms).

HAVE KIDS FORM two teams, and have both teams line up on one side of the room. Give the first person on each team a yardstick. (If you don't have yardsticks, use mops or brooms.) Have the Yardstick Holders stand five feet away from their teams and hold the yardstick like a cane, with one end in their hands and the other end on the floor.

Say: **On "go," Yardstick Holders will yell out the name of the first person on their team, then will immediately let go of the yardstick. The person whose name was called has to grab the yardstick before it falls to the ground. If the person misses, he or she goes to the end of the line, and the Yardstick Holder yells out the name of the next team member. If that person catches the yardstick before it hits the ground, he or she becomes the Yardstick Holder and calls out the next team member's name. Each team continues until everyone has had a chance to catch the stick. Ready? Go!**

After the relay, keep a yardstick with you when you return to your meeting. Periodically throughout the meeting, stand near someone then call out his or her name as you let the yardstick drop. See if that person can catch the stick before it hits the ground. ✺

 99 Penny-Pinching

You'll need two pennies.

HAVE KIDS FORM two teams, and have both teams line up on one side of the room. Give a penny to the first person on each team. Say: **Penny pinchers, lean your head back and place the penny on the tip of your nose. On "go," walk across the room and back, balancing the penny on your nose. When you return to the line, remove the penny from your nose using only one fingertip. Balance the penny on your fingertip, then transfer it to the next team member's fingertip. That person must balance the penny on a fingertip, place the penny on his or her nose, and balance the penny while walking across the room and back. If the penny drops, you have to go back to the front of the line and start over again. If the penny drops while you're transferring it to the next team member, pick it up, then start the transfer over again. Any questions? Ready? Go!**

Applaud the penny-pinching participants, collect the pennies, then go on with the meeting. ✺

100 Peg Leg

HAVE KIDS FORM four teams, and assign each team a corner of the room. Have each team turn a chair upside down in its corner.

Say: **Each team will try to "peg" the legs of its chair by tossing items that will hook on and stay in place. You must hook four items per leg. "Hookable" items might include key chains, headbands, plastic cups, shoes, and so on.**

When your team has pegged all legs, shout, "Peg leg!" Ready? Let's go!

When the game is over, have teams compare the items they pegged. Have teams return the chairs to their original positions, then have kids return to their seats. ☺

101 Making a Scene

You'll need a Bible.

IF YOUR KIDS need a change of scene from the routine, try this creative activity. Form teams of six to eight kids. Say: **I'll read a passage from Proverbs. As a team, decide how to make a "human scene" to represent those verses. You can use props from around the room.**

Read Proverbs 24:3-4: **"It takes wisdom to have a good family, and it takes understanding to make it strong. It takes knowledge to fill a home with rare and beautiful treasures."**

If kids are having a hard time creating a scene, offer some suggestions. For example, one team could form a circle (symbolizing the home or family) and could have one person read the Bible (symbolizing wisdom), another stand in a "muscleman" pose (symbolizing strength), another kneel in *The Thinker* pose (symbolizing knowledge), and the rest holding such things as jewelry, flowers, or art objects (symbolizing rare and beautiful treasures). Another idea could be for kids to build a three-tiered human pyramid (to symbolize family and strength), to place a Bible on each level (to symbolize wisdom and knowledge), and to place valuable things, such as jewelry or ornamental items, at the top (to symbolize beautiful treasures).

Read the passage several times while kids are creating their scenes. When both teams are done, applaud their artistic efforts. Say: **Let's continue to build a foundation of wisdom by getting back to our meeting.** ☺

102 One, Two, Pass

You'll need scrap paper.

HAVE EVERYONE form a circle and number off by twos. Randomly pick a "one" person, and give him or her a wad of scrap paper. On the opposite side of the circle, give a "two" person a wad of scrap paper.

Say: **When I say, "One, two, pass," the "one" person will pass the paper wad to the next "one" on his or her right, who will pass the paper wad to the next "one" on his or her right, and so on. At the same time, the "two" person will pass the paper wad to the next "two" on his or her right, who will pass it to the next "two," and so on.** (See illustration.)

The object of the race is to pass the paper quickly, so you can catch up to the other team's paper. Ready? One, two, pass!

Play several rounds, reversing directions each time. Say: OK, time to "pass" on this game. Let's get back to our meeting. 🔅

103 Get Hopping

You'll need paper.

DOES YOUR lesson need a jump-start? Get kids hopping with this fun relay. Lay twelve sheets of paper on the floor in two rows, placing six sheets in each row. The sheets should be one foot apart, and rows should be six feet apart. Have kids form two teams, and have each team line up behind a row of paper.

Say: **When I say "go," the first person on each team must hop backward over each sheet of paper in that row, then hop forward to the front, and then tag the next person in line. That person will repeat the procedure, and the next person, until everyone in line has hopped.**

If time allows, play again and have kids hop on one foot. Applaud all the hoppers and say: **I'm "hoppy" to see that everyone is having such a good time. But now we need to return to our lesson, so let's all hop back to our seats.** Ask for a volunteer to hop over and pick up the paper and then hop back to his or her seat. 🌀

104 The Book Stops Here

You'll need a book.

HAVE KIDS FORM a circle. Hand someone a book and say: **Quickly pass the book from person to person around the circle as I count, "One, two, three, four, five." When I get to five, the person holding the book has to name five people in the group before he or she can continue passing the book. We'll continue like this, with everyone quickly passing the book as I count to five. Ready?**

Start counting. Continue the game until several people have held the book and have named five group members. Stop counting to end the game and say: **OK, the book stops here. Let's get back to our meeting.** 🌀

105 Twist My Arm

You'll need chalkboard erasers and trash cans.

HAVE KIDS FORM three teams, and have each team stand in a line. Give the first person in each line an empty trash can. Have him or her hold the trash can waist-high, walk five feet in front of the line, then turn around and face the rest of the team. Give each team a chalkboard eraser.

Say: **We're going to have a relay called Twist My Arm. Each team member will get three chances to throw the eraser into his or her team's trash can. The catch is that when it's your turn, you must turn around so your back is facing the trash can. You can look over your shoulder to aim, but you can't turn your body around; you must keep your back to the trash can. After everyone on your team has thrown the eraser, sit down. Ready? Go!**

After the relay is over, applaud all participants. Then say: **Great job! What a terrific twisted-arm effort. Now let's change aim and get back to our lesson.**

106 Brainstorm

You'll need paper and pencils.

DO YOU WANT to create some intellectual thunder? Exercise your kids' creativity with this quick pick-them-upper. Have kids form groups of no more than four. Give each group a sheet of paper and a pencil. Say: **Think of a quick, easy game that would be fun to play. Games can be anything: treasure hunts, human building blocks, tongue twisters, whistling contests, freeze frame scenes...whatever you can think of. The only rules are that each game can only last five minutes and that the "equipment" has to be something that's already in our meeting room. You'll get five minutes to come up with a game. Write your idea on your sheet of paper. When I call time, be prepared to explain your game to the rest of us.**

After five minutes, call time, and have kids briefly explain their games to each other. Then send the games to the following address for possible inclusion in another snore-dom-busting games book.

Group Publishing, Inc.
Product Development Dept.
Box 481
Loveland, CO 80539
ATTN: Youth Editor

Evaluation of *Group's Snore-dom™ Busters*

Please help Group Publishing, Inc., continue to provide innovative and usable resources for ministry by taking a moment to fill out and send us this evaluation. Thanks!

● ● ●

1. As a whole, this book has been (circle one):

Not much help   Very helpful

1   2   3   4   5   6   7   8   9   10

2. The things I liked best about this book were:

3. This book could be improved by:

4. One thing I'll do differently because of this book is:

5. Optional Information:

Name _____

Street Address _____

City _____ State _____ Zip _____

Phone Number _____ Date _____